William Tell

WILLIAM TELL

Retold and illustrated
by
Margaret Early

Harry N. Abrams, Inc., Publishers, New York

A LONG TIME AGO, beside the shores of Lake Lucerne, high in the mountains of Europe, were three tiny countries: Schwytz, Uri, and Unterwalden. These lands, of breathtaking beauty, were blessed with fertile fields, lush meadows, and streams abundant with fish, and forests rich with game.

The people of Schwytz, Uri, and Unterwalden were happy, prosperous and contented — until the day they lost their freedom to Austria, their large and powerful neighbour. From that moment they were forced to pay heavy and unjust taxes to the Austrian Emperor's soldiers and Governors, who occupied the lands and ruled their new subjects through cruelty and terror.

Everyone lived in fear of the foreign tyrants, the worst of whom was an evil Governor named Gessler. A harsh dictator, he ordered his Austrian soldiers to destroy the animals and crops and burn down the houses of anyone who dared to disobey his commands.

AT ALTDORF Gessler ordered a stronghold — the Uri Keep — to be erected. The men who were forced to build it did so with heavy hearts, for they knew that one day it would become their own prison, the graveyard of their freedom.

Gessler was always thinking of new ways to torment his unhappy subjects. One day he had his hat placed on a pole in the middle of a public place, and instructed his soldiers to make everyone pay homage to it. On bended knee, and with uncovered head, the people had to bow down before the hat, as though the hat were Gessler himself.

Two soldiers stood on guard to make sure every passer-by bowed, but most people cunningly avoided the hat when going about their daily business, even if it meant having to walk halfway round Altdorf to do so.

HE EDICT that everyone must bow down before an empty hat made the people angry. One night, the chief men of the three countries held a secret meeting on the Rütli, a meadow by a wood, high above the lake. Here they swore an oath — known as the Rütli Oath — to join together in a plan to regain their freedom. On New Year's Eve they would storm the castles of the foreign Governors and, as each was taken, fires would be lit on the hills as a sign for the rest of the people to rise up and rid their lands of the Austrian tyrants.

The chiefs were amazed when a rainbow suddenly appeared in the moonlit sky. 'This is a strange and wondrous sight,' they said. 'Surely, it is a sign from heaven that we will be delivered from our cruel oppressors? If we unite as one people, we cannot fail.'

I N THE MOUNTAINS above Altdorf lived William Tell, with his wife Hedwig and their two sons, Walter and Willi. No-one loved his family or his country or his freedom more than Tell, and none was more skilled as a marksman and hunter.

One morning Tell said to Walter, 'Would you like to go with me to Altdorf today to visit your grandmother and grandfather?'

'Oh, yes, please, Father,' said Walter eagerly. 'May Willi come, too?'

'He can stay and keep your mother company. We will bring him back a present.'

When Hedwig heard this, she pleaded with her husband not to go to Altdorf, because the despised Governor would surely be there.

'Have no fear, dear wife,' Tell assured her. 'Gessler has no reason to harm us. We will be back safely by nightfall.'

But Hedwig knew that Gessler was jealous of the respect the people gave to Tell, and that he might regard her husband as a threat to his own power.

ELL WALKED down the mountain track, hand-in-hand with Walter, who was excited at the thought of seeing his grandparents again. Walter was also a little worried, lest his mother's fears come true. He had heard that Gessler needed only the smallest excuse to punish innocent people.

When they arrived in Altdorf they saw the hat on the pole, but they did not know what it meant, for they had not yet heard of Gessler's new law. As father and son walked past the pole without bowing down, one of the guards drew his sword. 'You have not shown reverence to the Governor's hat,' he shouted. 'You have disobeyed his command, so you must now pay the penalty of imprisonment — or death.'

'I am a free man,' Tell replied proudly. 'I willingly bow my head before God, or the Emperor himself, but I will not do reverence to an empty hat.'

At that very moment Gessler arrived on horseback, fresh from hunting, just in time to overhear Tell's declaration of defiance.

ESSLER POINTED to William Tell accusingly. 'It is because you despise your Emperor and your Governor that you refuse to respect the hat,' he said. 'For that you must be punished.'

'Forgive me,' said Tell, 'but I had no knowledge of your proclamation. Even so, I cannot believe that you expect people to bow down before an empty hat.'

Gessler glared angrily at Tell. 'I am a kind man,' he said, 'so I will give you a chance to prove yourself. I hear that you are renowned for your skill as an archer . . .'

'That is true,' interrupted Walter. 'My father can shoot an apple from a tree at fifty paces.'

'If you are such a fine marksman, Tell,' replied Gessler, 'let me see you shoot an apple from your son's head. If you succeed, you shall both go free — but if you fail, the punishment is death.'

HEN HE HEARD THIS, Tell was struck with horror, but Walter stepped forward and declared boldly, 'My father never misses. He can even shoot a bird in flight.'

Gessler ordered the boy to be blindfolded and bound to a tree, but Walter refused. 'I am not afraid of my father's arrow,' he said. 'I will stand firm while he shoots.'

The villagers were aghast. 'How can we permit such a monstrous crime to be committed before our eyes?' they muttered to each other. 'Was the Rütli Oath taken in vain? Have we all sworn defiance for nothing?'

Gessler knew that the villagers were longing to attack him, but he saw that they were unarmed, so he felt safe with his own soldiers around him.

Suppressing his anger, William Tell took two arrows from his quiver. He hid one inside his jerkin before fitting the other to his crossbow.

Slowly . . . carefully . . . he took aim . . .

T HE ONLOOKERS became silent: the branches of the trees swayed gently in the breeze, but there was no other sound to be heard. Walter stood firm and unflinching, hardly daring to breathe, willing his father to shoot straight and true.

Gathering all his strength and courage, Tell paused a moment — and then released the arrow. It sped through the air and found its target, piercing the apple to its very core.

Walter cried out in triumph as the apple fell to the ground. Seizing it, he ran to his father's arms, while the townsfolk embraced each other and cheered.

Gessler was speechless: he was angry that his plan had not worked, but was awe-struck by the skill of this simple mountain huntsman, and the bravery of his trusting son.

S WALTER AND HIS FATHER were about to walk away, surrounded by townsfolk, Gessler called out: 'One moment, Tell. That was very clever, I admit, but before I let you go there is something you must explain. I am curious to know why you hid a second arrow in your jerkin . . .'

Tell gazed calmly and fearlessly at Gessler. 'Had my aim been false, and I had killed my son, that arrow would have been aimed at your heart — and I would not have missed,' he said.

Gessler was furious. He ordered his soldiers to arrest Tell, saying, 'I promised your life would be spared if you succeeded in shooting the apple from your son's head. This promise I shall keep. Your son is free to return to his mother, but to save myself from your arrows I intend to have you thrown in the deepest, darkest dungeon of my castle across the lake. As long as you live, you will be my prisoner.'

Walter clung desperately to his father, and begged Gessler for mercy, but the soldiers wrenched him away and led their captive off to Gessler's waiting boat, leaving Walter to climb the mountain, bearing news that his mother's worst fears had come to pass.

A S HE SAT, bound and captive in Gessler's boat, William Tell thought about his future life. Never again would he see the light of sun or moon. Never again would he roam his beloved forests and mountains. Never again would his dear wife and children greet him at the end of the day.

Suddenly a bitter wind swept across the lake. Black clouds lowered, and lightning and thunder flashed and crashed around the boat. Rain teemed down from above, and the storm grew so fierce that the oarsmen soon lost heart — there was no safe harbour to be seen, only gigantic cliffs looming into the darkness above.

Knowing of Tell's great strength and skill as a helmsman, Gessler cried, 'Help us, Tell! If you can bring us all safely ashore you may have your freedom. Help us, before it is too late!'

With his ropes quickly untied, Tell seized his chance and took control of the wildly pitching vessel.

ELL STEERED THE BOAT towards a large rock which jutted out from a cliff. Suddenly, without a word, he snatched up his bow and quiver, leaped upwards to the rock, and with one foot thrust the boat back into the stormy lake.

Gessler sprang from his seat, but a great wave heaved the boat aloft and threw him down again. Without its helmsman, the helpless craft was tossed feebly on the raging waters.

Tell now climbed to the top of the cliff and to safety. As the storm began to subside, he planned to lie in wait for Gessler, should the boat somehow find its way ashore. He was familiar with all the paths and byways, and knew that there was only one approach to Gessler's castle — a track that led through a deep and narrow gorge, with thick bushes on either side. Here Tell would hide himself and wait for the despised Governor to appear.

A S HE LAY IN WAIT for his enemy, William Tell thought of his wife and children. Their lives would now be in great danger, for Gessler would surely kill them in revenge.

It was not long before the evil Governor and his men rode up the path. As Tell watched, a peasant woman suddenly appeared and threw herself on her knees before the tyrant. Her husband had been unjustly imprisoned and she had come to plead for his freedom.

Gessler was unmoved by the woman's passionate cries. 'Get out of my way, you vile beggar,' he snarled, raising his arm to strike her.

At that moment Tell drew his bow and arrow, took aim, and fired. True to his word, he did not miss.

Gessler fell from his horse, shot through the heart.

HE NEWS OF GESSLER'S DEATH quickly spread from village to village. Bells rang out, and fires were lit on mountaintops to let people know that the time had come to rise up against their oppressors. Before long, the castles of the Governors were on fire, and the Austrian soldiers were fleeing the land.

In Altdorf, men began tearing down the Uri Keep, while children danced around the hat on the pole. Instead of burning it, the villagers decided to keep it as a symbol of their victory.

'But where is William Tell?' they asked. 'Let us go to his house and show our thanks for what he has done for his people and his country.'

ELL'S WIFE AND CHILDREN waited anxiously for his return. At last they saw him approaching, and Walter and Willi ran to greet him, with joy in their hearts.

How happy they were to be reunited with their father again!

'But, Father, where is your crossbow?' asked Willi.

'My kinsmen have taken it, to preserve it as a memento of our victory and liberation,' Tell replied.

Then the sound of alpenhorns could be heard in the distance. Coming up the valley towards the house were the people of Altdorf. When they saw Tell they cheered him and gave thanks. 'It is through your example of courage and bravery that we have been shown the way to restore freedom to our beloved land,' they told him, while Hedwig and Walter and Willi looked on with pride.

Later, the people of Schwytz, Uri, and Unterwalden met on the shore of Lake Lucerne and resolved to become one free, united country which would be large enough and strong enough to stand up for itself and protect its freedom, for ever more.

They decided to call their new country Switzerland and, to this day, the Swiss people have never forgotten the brave deeds of their hero, William Tell.

To Phyllis Shillito and Aytoun Young
— M.E.

Library of Congress Catalog Card Number: 91-70686
ISBN 0–8109–3854–5
Text and illustrations copyright © 1991 Margaret Early
First published in Australia in 1991 by Walter McVitty Books
Published in 1991 by Harry N. Abrams, Incorporated, New York
A Times Mirror Company
Printed and bound in Hong Kong